MASTER GUIDE

HOW TO PROFIT WITH POKEMON

How to profit with Pokemon

This is a step-by-step training guide on how to profit with Pokemon.

No part of this book may be used or reproduced in any manner whatsoever without written permission except in the case of brief quotations embodied in critical articles, books and reviews.

CONTENTS

Investing	Page 1
Ripping	Page 9
Grading	Page 12
Bulk	Page 15
Languages	Page 16
Purchasing, Selling & Identifying Scams	Page 19
Pokemon Wizardry	Page 27

Investing

Welcome to the Master Guide of making money with Pokemon. We're going to assume you already know what Pokemon is and understand there's money making potential within it, so we can skip the explanation and get right to work.

The first question anyone asked themselves when considering starting a business is "Is it profitable?". Making money with Pokemon can be done in many different ways and we will explain some unique ways you may not have heard of or thought about, but the short answer is yes, you can profit with Pokemon.

Before we get into the raw skills to build and scale a profitable Pokemon business, let's look at the simple form of investing in Pokemon. It's true that every single Pokemon booster pack and booster box that released before 2015 is worth more today that it was on its release date. This is true even in down markets.

Buying Pokemon products at retail and holding them is almost a full-proof strategy to profit if your plan is long-term investment. There are many specific sets that you should prioritize over others, which we will share in this guide. Having said that, there's not a single Pokemon booster pack or booster box that was released between 1996 and 2015 that's not increased in value. Even the most unpopular sets (Steam Siege, cough cough) increase in value over time.

Let's say you have $10,000 you want to invest for the longterm. Looking at Pokemon purely from a numbers perspective, and combining that with the knowledge of which sets to buy, there's actually not that many investments that can trump Pokemon.

Let's say you invest your $10,000 in the S&P, stock market, or another platform or asset that produces a consistent 7% per year. If you're lucky enough to find such a stable investment, you don't touch your money and leave it to compound, here's what that will look like over a 10 year period;

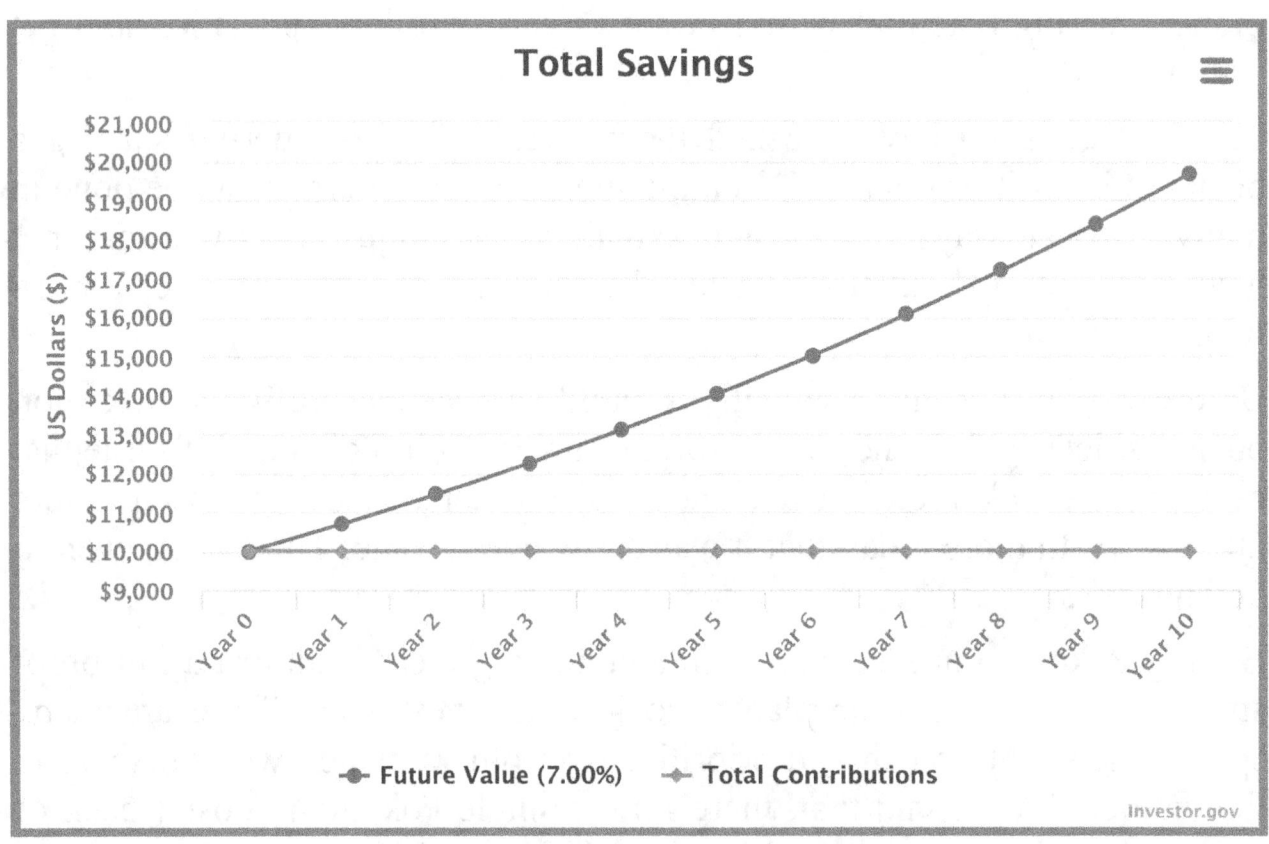

Let's break this investment down year by year and then compare it to historic Pokemon prices and investments.

$10,000 investment with 7% yearly interest. After;

Year 1 - $10,700
Year 2 - $11,449
Year 3 - $12,250
Year 4 - $13,107
Year 5 - $14,025
Year 6 - $15,007
Year 7 - $16,057
Year 8 - $17,181
Year 9 - $18,384
Year 10 - $19,671

This shows the growth over a 10 year period while compounding your interest and not touching your money. You can see how your investment would look should you choose to withdraw it at any point over the 10 year period. It would take 11 years to double your money, providing nothing went wrong.

Now let's look at three Pokemon sets and see how that $10,000 investment could do with them. We'll focus on booster boxes for this example. We're going to share the three sets that we've invested in over the recent years. Please note, all of these were purchased at retail. This chart will show the year of release and the value today, based on a $10,000 investment.

This chart shows an investment of 70 Booster boxes @ $142 each, totaling an overall investment (at retail price) of $10,000.

You can then see the current market price of 70 booster boxes for each set;

	7% Annual ROI	Plasma Blast (2013)	Evolutions (2016)	Team Up (2019)	Evolving Skies (2021)
Year 1	$10,700	2014	2017	2020	$12,950
Year 2	$11,449	2015	2018	2021	$18,900
Year 3	$12,250	2016	2019	$63,000	
Year 4	$13,107	2017	2020	$70,000	
Year 5	$14,025	2018	2021		
Year 6	$15,007	2019	$56,910		
Year 7	$16,057	2020	$49,000		
Year 8	$17,181	2021			
Year 9	$18,834	2022			
Year 10	$19,671	$154,000			

As you can see with even newer sets, like Evolving Skies, you can make a much higher ROI on Pokemon than traditional investments. In just the first 12 months you've increased your investment by 30% and in year two that grows to 89%. Of course, the longer you hold, the more they will be worth.

Every Pokemon set eventually goes out of print, whether that's a few months or a few years. When it does, the price of the set will naturally increase. So, if it's this easy, why doesn't everyone do it?

Many people do, but there are some clear reasons why people don't capitalize on this hugely profitable investment.

Lack of control

Almost everyone who invests in Pokemon is not doing so without emotion. If it was a clear mathematical decision, then this wouldn't be a reason, but that's not the case. Most people who invest are going to be tested every single day they look at their Pokemon collection and it's a constant war going on in their mind as to whether or not they should open them.

Whether or not there's a chase card in one of the packs.

Pokemon didn't grow from logical investors. It grew from children having an emotional response to the excitement of the cards and the increased dopamine release in their brains when they opened packs, both from the thrill of the chase and finding their desired card(s).

This emotional response hasn't dissipated much in adulthood, either. The thrill of the chase and the possibility of finding your desired card is still an emotional response adults have, as well as increased levels of dopamine. This is why many Pokemon fans of all ages open the packs they'd planned to save for the long term.

Finances

A lot of Pokemon fans who purchase products for long term investments may run into financial difficulties or need to raise money for an emergency. We've seen it time and time again where people will sell their "investment" after only a few short months to raise money for something. This isn't a tactical move because the product is still selling around retail, so it's clear to see they are in need of funds.

"Scalpers"

There's a huge difference between an investor and a scalper. An investor is everything we have described above. Having knowledge of the market and what they are buying with a clear plan to profit over the long term. A scalper goes and recklessly buys Pokemon at retail price hoping there will be a shortage of stock so they can sell it for more. We do teach a course on retail arbitrage and flipping, but this is more targeted towards finding products that can be flipped consistently and blurring the lines between affiliate programs. Scalping is slightly different. It's buying everything you can off the shelves and spinning around to sell it for a few dollars more, showcasing to your customers that you're blatantly clearing the shelves, thus customers having to pay more. Having said this, we're not against the process, but we will never participate in it. We don't like the idea of parents having to hunt multiple stores just to get their kids a pack of Pokemon cards, potentially leading some to just abandon the hobby due to the only being able to buy at higher prices. Secondly, it's just not very profitable.

Scalping prevents investors buying at retail and many just won't buy from a "scalper" because they know they're just being charged more by someone trying to benefit from low stock levels.

Space

Pokemon collecting can take up a good amount of space, especially if you're investing a considerable amount of money. Using the figure we mentioned earlier of $10,000, this will get you around 70 booster boxes at retail. That's a pretty substantial amount of space that's required to house your investment, so people let go of their sealed product simply for this reason.

There are other reasons as well, from damage to unpaid storage units.

Now, if you have an investor who put their money into Pokemon and avoided any reason for opening or selling them, including avoiding damaging them, then sure... The chances are they will be extremely profitable when purchasing the correct sets.

Finally, we'd like to share some of the sets that have caught our attention for long-term investment. Though this is not financial advise and we suggest doing your own research, these are the recent products we are confident will provide the best ROI. We've put the current market price so you can see if we are wrong in a couple of years;

Flashfire Sleeved Booster Packs - $55

Celebrations Elite Trainer Box - $80

Evolving Skies Booster Box - $278

Evolving Skies Triple Blister Pack - $35

Brilliant Stars Booster Box - $184

VSTAR Universe Box (Japanese) - $92

Pokemon Center Exclusive products (at retail)

When it comes to investing in Pokemon for the long term, we try to avoid the soft card boxes, such as Lance's Charizard Celebrations Box (even though we believe this is a good investment as well) because they're big and bulky and can be damaged very easily.

We typically stick to booster boxes, sleeved booster packs, and blister packs. It's far less hassle later down the line when you finally decide to sell. If you're trying to sell a $200 loose booster pack, there are customer concerns focused on whether the pack has been weighed and whether it's been resealed. The amount of people whom have been scammed just from these two examples is baffling.

With sealed booster boxes, sleeved booster packs and triple blisters, there's almost no resistance when it comes to concern of weighed packs and people won't be concerned with packs being opened and resealed.

The last tip we want to share is protecting your investment. Sure, put it in a safe, secure location, but we're referring to protective casing. You can purchase acrylic cases for ETBs and booster boxes. Although they're $20-$25 a unit, that could be a very good investment for the long term. A $2,000 booster box could easily drop more than $25 in value if it got damaged.

There's similar products available for sleeved booster packs and triple boosters. You may also consider buying sealed cases of these products as the condition of the exterior box having a few scratches or a small dent in the corner doesn't after the market value as much as it would if it were a damaged booster box.

Ripping

Walk into a LCS (Local Card Store), buy a $3.99 booster pack, hit a $200 card, grade it, get a Black Label, sell it for $4,000. Easy right? Although this has been the reality for some people, this outcome is pure luck and most will never experience this.

If you're skipping long term investing or doing a combination of strategies, one of them will probably be "ripping". This is the terminology used for opening Pokemon packs. You'll be opening packs to search for the chase cards and profit from doing this.

When you start out with lower volume, luck plays a huge factor in profit, but as you scale your business and start opening ten of thousands of packs, you'll begin to hit the averages for Pokemon's print runs and remove luck altogether.

If you open one booster box (36 packs), you may hit some fire or you may bust, but if you open 100 booster boxes (3,600 packs) you're going to start balancing out the good and the bad and begin getting the averages. At 100 booster boxes you're going to be at enough volume to complete master sets. This is basically one of every card. Some business owners choose to use this strategy and aim to complete a master set, sell it, and the duplicates can then be sold individually or graded.

Sure, if you were to sell every card individually you'd probably net a little more profit, but at that level, you're probably in it for the bigger bucks and don't want to mess around selling reverse holos and frequently found V cards.

Your strategy for what happens with the Pokemon cards you open will heavily depend on your financial capacity. For example, if you're sixteen years old with only $20 available then you're probably going to sell all cards individually to maximize profits. At the other end of the spectrum, you may have significantly better starting capital and choose to buy 100 booster boxes. At this level, your time is going to be worth far more than the profit from individually selling reverse holos.

There is one situation where someone opening huge volume may choose to sell individual cards and that's if they have a website or a store and they want to stock as many cards as possible. Even at $0.25 a card, if you're selling thousands, it's going to be significantly more profitable than selling them as "bulk", something we'll come to later. Ultimately, it's up to you to calculate how much your time is worth and considered the work that it would take to individually sell low value cards.

Moving onto the business and the numbers, the main question to answer is whether or not it's profitable to open packs and sell raw cards for profit. These answer is maybe. It goes back to volume. If you're opening small volume then luck is going to play a relatively large role. Maybe you hit the monster pulls or maybe you hit nothing.

If you're purchasing sleeved booster packs from multiple sources then you are playing a riskier game, but this may also yield a higher reward. Where as if you purchase a booster box, you're going to **typically** have at least a few hits. At huge volume, this also balances out and your goal is to acquire product that translates to the lowest cost per pack, which is typically booster boxes.

Unfortunately, until you reach the higher volumes there's no real guarantee of pulls at all, though you'll usually hit something pretty solid in your first 30 or so packs.

There's a good chunk of data available online from people reporting their pull rates from a few thousand packs which can be useful information for those of you planning to open high volume. Outside of volume, you could get absolutely anything. We've had our team open batches of cards across many small volume situations. We've opened three sleeved booster packs and pulled two copies of the #1 chase card in the set (Lost Origin) and also opened 50 packs and got nothing beyond a V card. Again, over thousands of packs, it always balances out. We've never opened a 5,000 pack batch and had anything out of the ordinary in terms of pull rates.

When opening packs, it's best to handle them with care and consider that you may be about to come across a chase card. Our opening strategy may be considered overkill, but we don't ever touch the face of the cards with our hands. Once we open a fan and gently fan it out, we then put any chase cards directly into a penny sleeve by only holding the edges of the card. Just being observant over the fact that condition is important will suffice, though.

Once you've opened your packs and sleeved your cards, it's time to figure out what to do with each category. We sort out cards into these categories, but you may choose a slightly different variation;

Bulk; Common, Uncommon, Reverse Holo

Mid Tier; V, VMAX, VSTAR

Top Tier; Rainbow, Secret Rare, Gold

Chase Cards; Typically Alt Arts (the most valuable in the set)

Grading

One of the options you'll have after you've ripped packs open, in addition to selling raw cards, is grading. Though most people stick to the big three, we'll share an expanded list of card graders from multiple countries. When it comes to grading, volume results in inconsistency and sometimes lower quality.

We're not here to throw stones at companies, but we've seen graded cards that are so inconsistent, it's comical. We've seen cards graded in a 10 with blatant off-centering and roughed edges and other cards that should be sitting at an easy 10, but only getting an 8.

Though the big three are the go-to for most people, the newer and smaller graded shouldn't be ignore as they tend to have far better quality control prior to scaling and taking on hoards of staff that may not share the same passion as the owner.

So, what is grading? It's simply having a "grading company" encapsulate your Pokemon cards for a few reasons. To identify it's grade (quality), showcase it and preserve its condition. Grading is relatively similar across the board, meaning a 10 from one company is typically going to get a 10 with another company. However, this can vary depending on which companies you're comparing as some are stricter than others and each individual grader within the company may have their own varying range for each grade.

Grading your cards typically increases the price of the card. We say typically because if you have a $200 card and it grades in a 6 or 7, then there's a good chance it can fall below the raw price. Though you should also consider that in recent years people will pay less for a card that shows obviously signs that it'll get a low grade. Before moving on, here's a list of some of the available grading companies you can submit card to;

PSA (Professional Sports Authenticators) – US, Hong Kong, Japan

BGS (Beckett Grading Services) – US

CGC (Comic Grading Company) – US

HGA (Hybrid Gaming Approach) – US

SGC – US

PG (PokeGrade) – UK

PCA Grading – Europe

CGA (Card Grading Australia) – Australia

GP (Golden Prestige) – Dubai

PCG (Platinum Card Grading) - UK

There was an influx of new grading companies established in recent years because people identified an opportunity when the big three (PSA, BGS, and CGC) has a severe backlog due to the pandemic. They have since cleared their backlog and are back to full speed, though this back log opened the door for many new companies to form, some of which are actually gaining traction.

Once you've decided on which grading company to use, the next step, which is sometimes more difficult, is deciding which cards to submit. There are a few things to factor in when making this decision and that includes; cost per card, timeline and transitional value. If it costs $25 to grade a card, then sending in a common card is not going to be profitable.

The timeline is the service you choose (most grading companies have many options based on price and processing time) and it can take days or months to have your graded cards returned base on which option you choose. If you're grading high value cards, then the difference between $25 and $40 a card may not be a huge factor, though this cost can rack up at volume. You also have to consider if you're in a rush to get your cards back so you can sell them quickly to reinvest in your business.

Transitional value is the difference between the cost of the card raw and the cost of the card when it is graded. Factor in what grade you think the card is going to receive (most grading companies' grading system is public on their sites) and the transitional price from raw to graded.

There's a few tools you can use to get graded prices such as eBay, the Pokemon Almanac book and other websites. Just be aware that the faster you get cards graded from a new set, the less data there will be. This can work with you or against you because the prices can drastically change over the month's following a set's release. One example of this would be the "Moonbreon" from Evolving Skies. It was floating between $150-$180 in Fall 2021 and within a few months the price tripled and held at the $450 range. The opposite example would be the Special Delivery Charizard that was given away to random customers by Pokemon Center on their website. At its peak it was selling comfortably for $150-$200. You can pick one up in early 2023 for $40, sealed.

BULK

A very common question, especially for new Pokemon collectors and sellers is what they should do with their bulk. This usually refers to common, uncommon and sometimes rare non-holos and reverse holos.

Energy cards are usually considered more trash than bulk, but you may wish to hold onto them and store them away for a few decades. The 1st Edition Base Energy cards from 1999 that have been graded in a PSA 10 are going for over $70 each. We'll leave that decision to you.

Organizing your bulk cards depends on the scale of your business. If you're ripping packs to find chase cards and grade them with no interest in anything under a VMAX or VSTAR, then you'll probably be throwing common, uncommon, rare, and reverse holo into your bulk. If you don't have the ability to open larger volumes you may wish to sell the rare holos and reverse holos to maximize profits, as mentioned before. Again, if you're trying to list and stock as many cards as possible, including commons, then you may not have any bulk to sell.

If you do have bulk to clear out, the best way to sell it is probably going to be your LCS (Local Card Shop/Store) as you'll avoid having to ship. One tip if you're opening larger volumes and know you'll have a consistent supply of bulk is to shop around and see where you're going to get the best rates, whether than be a LCS or one of the other sales platforms, we will share later.

You can also give it away to schools and charities, but even if you're operating at the higher echelons of business, at $15 per 1,000, that'll mount up if you open 5,000 packs a week (30,000 cards @ $15/1,000 = $450).

Languages

Though most Pokemon fans focus primarily on English sets, there's a huge market in foreign cards as well. It's also a much more niche market. Pokemon release sets in many different languages including;

English, Spanish, Portuguese, German, Thai, Chinese, Korean, Indonesian, and of course Japanese. If you were to think of Pokemon as a currency, the two most valuable would definitely be English and Japanese, which is why they are the most heavily traded languages.

The important thing to note is that each language often release artworks that are not obtainable in other languages. You can date this back to the very first Pokemon cards ever released.

There's literally too many examples to list, but we'll share a few nice artworks that aren't available in any English set;

Pokemon Vending Series 1 & 2 (Japanese)

Charizard – 276/XY-P – XY Promo (Japanese)

Acerola – 201/200 - Dreams Come True AC2b (Chinese)

Lillie – 202/200 – Dreams Come True AC2b (Chinese)

In addition to country-exclusive artworks, there are also cards that fall into this category because they were banned, due to what people considered "explicit" artwork. A few examples of these are as follows;

Sabrina's Gengar – Challenge from the Darkness

The English set equivalent would be Gym Heroes, atleast that's the set that contains the English version. In the original Japanese artwork Gengar is standing in a graveyard and this artwork was ultimately banned, thus the English version was a plain background. This card, especially in perfect condition, is worth just shy of $100. Graded in a 10 it will surpass the $500 price tag quite easily.

Misty's Tears – Challenge from the Darkness

Another card from the Japanese same set was banned due to the artwork being too explicit for another reason. Misty is topless in the artwork and you can see the point of her breast, so it was banned. The English variation, which was in the Gym Challenge set, was a completely different design altogether and just showed a close-up of her face with Squirtle wiping her tear.

There's probably a conclusive list of the banned Japanese card artworks, but others include Grimer; Whose eye angle was perceived to be looking up a girl's skirt, and Golbat; With a blatant red swastika on the artwork.

Another difference with country-specific releases, at least in recent years, is the reverse holos and holo variants. If you look at the SWSH Celebrations Charizard from the English set, it's very different from the Asian release. The English card has a plain yellow border with the bulky glitter design in the holo section, where as the Asian release (Japanese, Chinese, Thai, etc) has a much finer glitter design with a full gold glitter border.

This example is region specific, but there's also other examples, such as the reverse holos in the Chinese sets. Just get your hands on the full art reverse holo Pikachu from the 25th anniversary collection in Chinese (yes there's a standard holo and reverse holo) and you'll see what we're talking about. It's pretty wild.

Having unique cards that most people either haven't seen in person or aren't aware of, can give you a competitive advantage in business. Imagine going to one of the large trading card shows and being the only vendor with some of these cards. Even if you didn't sell them, you'd certainly get attention and more eyes on your business.

Purchasing, Selling & Identifying Scams

Purchasing is one of the most important things for your business. You not only need peace of mind that you're getting authentic products from a licensed reseller every time, but you need a consistent flow of product. Of course it's obvious to try and find a distributor to do business with, but there's a few reasons you shouldn't rely solely on this strategy. The main reason being stock allocation. Distributors, at least the lower level ones, can frequently run out of stock as they're allocating a certain volume.

On top of that, many distributors boost their prices above retail, even at the wholesale level it can be hard to get good pricing. Some distributors don't even wholesale at all because they're happy to sell to the end line customer and capitalize on the margins.

We're going to share some buying platforms with you that'll provide you a collection of businesses where you can safely buy Pokemon without getting "scalped".

Amazon

There's a large shadow that's been cast over buying Pokemon from Amazon, and for good reason. That doesn't mean it's not a useful purchase platform if you know how to use it. And notice we said Amazon, not isolating Amazon.com.

Firstly, you should be aware that the majority of Amazon sites ship internationally. This can offer you access to many foreign cards.

Before we get into this, it's important to note that Amazon themselves sell Pokemon directly without having a third party seller involved. You can differentiate between whether the product is sold by Amazon or a third-party seller;

The top arrow points to "Ships from". This is the who's shipping the product. Third-party sellers can use FBA (Fulfillment by Amazon) which shows that Amazon ship's a products that's actually coming from a third-party seller. Be aware that Amazon ship both their own products as well as third-party sellers who use FBA.

The second arrow on the right points to the entity actually selling the item. If it's says "Amazon" in this section then you're buying directly from Amazon, but if it has the name of a third-party seller then you're not buying from Amazon, even though they're the ones shipping it.

Scammers use this technique to lure customers into a false sense of security assuming it's shipped from Amazon then it's safe and not a resealed pack. The issue is, Amazon just provide the FBA service and don't check if packs are authentic or resealed so they can quite easily be shipping packs that have been resealed.

Amazon do ship & sell Pokemon products themselves, so be aware whether you're buying a product directly from Amazon or from a third-party seller that's using FBA.

If you're in Mexico, the majority of Pokemon booster packs sold on the Amazon platform are actually shipped by Amazon themselves (Amazon.com.mx).

Remembering Amazon ship globally, you can also tap into other country-specific Amazon platforms. Here's a list;

US – Amazon.com

Canada – Amazon.ca

Mexico - Amazon.com.mx

UK – Amazon.co.uk

France – Amazon.fr

Germany – Amazon.de

Spain – Amazon.es

Italy – Amazon.it

Japan – Amazon.co.jp

You can use Google Chrome's auto-translator extensions to covert the sites into English or your chosen language.

Ebay

Using eBay's platform to purchase Pokemon is a great way to find a wide range of products at very competitive prices. The eBay market has become so competitive that it's forced distributors who sell on eBay to squash their margins in order to compete.

We share a complete start to finish training of eBay in our eBay Wizardry course (available at stockroomdeals.com), but the main things to look out for when purchasing on eBay is the volume they sell, their feedback rating (%) and their history.

Facebook Marketplace

This is a dangerous game, but if you're perspicacious then you can find good deals without getting scammed. Just be aware that investigating the seller, their feedback, history and personal profile can give you more information as to whether or not they're a legitimate business person or a scam artist selling resealed or counterfeit packs.

Facebook Group

This is one of the best places on the planet to do business. Investigating who you are buying from is a mandatory exercise each time you do business with a new person, but you have everybody tradings, buying and selling in Pokemon Facebook groups from customers, traders, scalpers, resellers, investors and licensed distributors. You can also find people selling collections of cards, sealed products, graded cards and much more.

LCS

Local Card Stores are a great place to find deals, trades, and sell off cards you need to clear out, including bulk. Almost every country will have have an LCS and the majority of cites around the world have them within a few miles. Though LCS have Pokemon distributor accounts, typically, you should be vigilant of the pricing as some will push the prices up far above retail. Remembering, they're not a super store that has a tiny portion of their profit coming from Pokemon. They're a Pokemon-specific store so they're going to maximize profits at every opportunity. You can still strike good deals with them if you're buying in bulk and this is a good purchase platform where you can get sealed cases and sealed booster boxes.

They may also stock vintage products.

The final benefit is that you don't have to pay shipping and you have the products in-hand at the moment of purchase.

These purchasing platforms are great worldwide examples and no matter what country you're in, all should be accessible to you. If you're looking to buy in other places, you can search which businesses you have in your country. Here's another list of places you can purchase Pokemon, either at retail or fairly close. These are physical stores and websites. Some of the physical stores also have websites.

Various – Pokemoncenter.com

Worldwide – stockroomdeals.com

US – BestBuy

US – Walmart

US – Target

US – GameStop

US – TCGPlayer.com

US – CVS Pharmacy

US – Walgreen Pharmacy

Mexico – 7Eleven Convenience Stores

Mexico – Walmart

Mexico – GamePlanet

UK – Game

UK – Argos

Germany (All of Europe) – CardMarket.com

Philippines – Lazada (Red Lazada Mall badge = Authentic)

Philippines (+ Other Asian countries) – Toys R' Us

Philippines – Toy Kingdom

Japan – Pokemon Center (Tokyo)

Thailand – Ubuy.co.th

Hong Kong – Ubuy.co.hk

Now we've covered a good amount of buying platforms, the next step is to learn where to sell your Pokemon cards. This may seem very simple, but there's actually a lot of detail that people overlook and this is the backbone of your business because it will directly affect revenue and profits. Sales cures all.

When deciding which sales platforms to use, there's two things you need to consider. Traffic and fees.

You can tap into an instant audience if you're willing to pay for it, but this can each a large percentage of your profit and then you also have to consider shipping costs. This isn't such an issue with high value cards or products, but if you're selling a $20 card or product, shipping it is going to be 15% of your revenue.

Using platforms like eBay and Amazon will get your products sold relatively quickly because of their vast amounts of traffic, but you're going to be paying approximately 12% on eBay and around that on Amazon as well. So let's break down some rough math for eBay to give you some numbers that most people overlook and wonder why their business fails.

Sale Price - $50

eBay fees – 12% ($6.00)

Shipping cost - $4.50

Packaging materials $0.50

From a $50 sale, you're only going to generate about $39 of revenue after the running costs. This may sound fine, but then you have to factor in your time as well as what you paid for the card/product.

Over the long term, fees are going to be a major cost for running an eBay store. This is why eBay generate $19M a day in revenue. They now own TCGPlayer as well so the fees there will probably go up over the coming months and years.

Choosing other platforms may result in less traffic thus less sales, but you'll save on fees. You can consider Facebook Marketplace, Facebook groups, and your country's online marketplaces. LCS are fine for selling bulk and certain products, but you'll never get market value for your cards because they're buying from you with the intention of flipping them so they need to make a good margin, especially with the overheads of running a physical store.

It's truly up to you which sales platform you choose and which best fits your needs, but one of the best ways to sell your cards, if you're planning on growing a long-term business, would be to have your own online store.

Though this may seem like a daunting tasks, it's far easier than you may think. You can use companies like Ecwid and Shopify that can get you an online store up and running in hours for very little cost. Most are even free for the first few products.

If you were to do this, you'd reduce your fees from the averaging 12% to zero. The only fee you'll pay is a 2.9% transaction fee to your credit card processor. We'd recommend Square.

The downside of your own store is you have to pay for your own traffic if you can't generate it organically. This can be an endless rabbit hole of financial hell for some people and eBay know this. Many will end up resulting to places like eBay because it provides a turn key audience. However, we can show you how to build an enormous customer base from eBay's traffic in our eBay Wizardry course.

Networking on social media platforms and making friends in the Pokemon groups and community can be a great way to start to build a customer base as well.

Social media and Google ads that direct traffic to your website can be a useful tool and when you pay for this marketing and get customers, you can retain their e-mail address and start to build your customer base and brand.

Pokemon Wizardry

Now you've got all the data on Pokemon it's time to look at some pretty aggressive money making strategies. Understand business is war and if you don't put the odds in your favor you'll be eaten alive. The techniques we're about to teach you are completely legal, but will give you some secret strategies that can give you a competitive advantage over your competition.

Bypassing Retail Limits

When purchasing from big name stores, you may run into "retail limits". This is where you're limited to purchasing only a certain amount of products. There's two ways you can bypass this because even if you're just starting out in your Pokemon venture, having a limit of buying 4 products is going to be a problem.

The first way to bypass this is to take friends and family in with you and have each of them purchase 4 products. If you take 5 people with you and each of them purchase a boxset, you now have 20 boxsets instead of 4.

You can also do this without the help of anyone else by separating your transactions and there's a couple of ways to do this.

The first is to buy the 4 product limit, go and put them in your car and go right back into the store and buy another 4.

The second way is to separate your transactions on the conveyor belt. You can literally take 12 or 16 or 20 Pokemon products to the checkout and separate them into groups of 4 products. When you pay for your 4 products, the next transaction will be considered a new transaction and the system won't show that a limit has been reached for a product group. The employees at the checkout either don't know or don't care. Just say you're buying 4 items for each family member for a Pokemon opening competition to see who pulls the best cards. Many stores with limits even state it's "Limit of 4 per transaction", not per customer. Meaning you're completely abiding by the rules of the store.

The most creative way to do this would be the self checkouts. You just scan 4 Pokemon products, pay for it, then do another 4, then another 4. If you're resulting to retail purchasing and the store has a limit, this can be a useful method to know.

Sale or Return (Consignment)

You may not be aware that there's a large number of LCS that will be open to a consignment deal. This is where the store allows you to showcase your products for sale in their store in exchange for a fee, typically a percentage. You're not only providing them with quality products for their store, but it costs them nothing and they generate money from your sales.

The idea here is to get deals with LCS that want a lower percentage that the cost of selling fees on eBay. For example, if you're paying 12% on eBay, plus shipping costs and you strike a deal with a LCS that wants only 10% of revenue from the sales, you're instantly saving 2% + a mountain of shipping fees.

This is also beneficial when it comes to being paid. You're not at the mercy of eBay's buyer protection policy that allows customers to file a case and get their money back. Many sellers have been scammed by this and many more have seen eBay refund a customer when they got the goods.

Zero Cost Marketing

This method can take some time to build up a base, but it can be extremely profitable and ultimately reduce your need for time and money that you'd put into marketing.

Partner with people and offer them a percentage of sales they generate. Make sure this percentage is lower than typical seller fees. If they don't have a store, they'll likely sell products for 5-10% commission. Show them that they can start making money without any cost by marketing your products and you'll give them a commission from each sale.

The benefit to you is you can pay a smaller percentage than you would on places like eBay and until they make a sale, it costs you $0.

Become the Casino

This strategy relates to grading. Bare with us, because there's a method to our madness. There's a big opportunity still open that only one business (SlabCave @ stockroomdeals.com) has identified.

We expect the moment we share this information, there'll be an explosion of new grading businesses forming, but that's PSA's problem.

As you're probably aware, PSA announced at the start of 2023 that they were increasing their bottom-line cost to grade cards up to $19 each and this only added to this opportunity. It will now cost $19 to grade a card and this pricing makes it absolutely impossible for people to grade common, uncommon, and rare non-holo cards (from recent series') and make a profit, even if they grade a 10. It also makes it extremely difficult to grade reverse holos and some ultra rares and still profit.

Common and uncommon cards from recent eras, graded in a 10, which sell for between $10-$20. Some can reach higher prices around the $30 mark if they're the OG trio evolutions (Charizard, Blastoise, Venusaur), Pikachu,

Eevee, etc., but the majority of the time, you're looking under $20. With the cost of grading the card at $19, this market has been completely removed from existence. There's never going to be graded master sets anymore because people just can't justify grading common and uncommon cards. Not even every card in a set is graded anymore because of this cost. There's a demand for graded common, uncommon, reverse holo and ultra rares, but now there'll be no supply. Can you see the opportunity yet?

If you wanted to capitalize on this opportunity then consider starting your own grading company, but not using the structure of the typical grading titans.

Offering a much lower price than $19 to grade cards would open the door for people to grade thousands of lower ends cards, and sure you could make money at volume, but we'd suggest grading the lower value cards in house from your own pulls and then selling them on the market.

It costs about $1 to grade a card when you reach volume purchasing and it's not terribly expensive to set up a grading business if you're resourceful. By grading your own pulls you can now have all these cards in slabs for $1 each. If you're selling them for $10-$20, that's a huge margin and let's address the elephant in the room. You've got no competition.

Just an idea if you're looking for a new business in the Pokemon industry. Maybe you could even look into grading jumbo cards or other sealed products.

Grading Arbitrage

The final thing we'd like to share is something that's been tried and tested, but (to the best of our knowledge) never shared. It's arbitrage with a twist. For a master guide in arbitraging, check here: http://bit.ly/3Womw5W

Retail arbitrage is the act of buying something for X and selling it right away for a profit. Well, this is the advanced version of retail arbitrage with graded Pokemon cards...

As you may be aware, the big three graders (PSA, BGS, CGC) are desirable to most people because of their credibility. You know that if you have a card graded by the big three, it's going to increase in value and also hold its value. But what if you could get a PSA 10 for significantly cheaper than the market price? We've found a way. And no one loses.

The key here is to understand that a card in a PSA 10 will be worth far more than a card graded in a 10 by a brand new or lesser known grading company. So, you buy the graded 10 from the lesser known company and break the slab. Then submit it into PSA.

Before making a purchase you should look at the lesser known company's grading system to make sure that the card you're buying that's graded in a 10 will qualify as a PSA 10. They usually will. You'll have to do your own search to identify large gaps in the price of a PSA slab vs a lesser known slab, but here's a few examples of instant retail arbitrage opportunities that we found in a few minutes on eBay sold listings;

SWSH Celebration Blastoise

SGC 10 – Sold for $30

PSA 10 – Sold for $80

Team Rocket Dark Dugtrio

MGC 8 – Sold for $14

PSA 8 – Sold for $40

VSTAR Universe Irida

SC 10 – Sold for $202

PSA 10 – Sold for $500

When you find a slab that's selling under market of a PSA 10, it may be an opportunity for you to jump on it. Factor in the cost of grading cards with PSA, Beckett or CGC. Even if you make a few dollars a unit, it's still money in for doing something you love and applying multiple techniques we've shared in this book will only generate greater income.

You can expand this technique even further buy sending flawless looking cards into Beckett and if they receive a Black Label, you're going to profit considerably more.

As you research and try more and more different variations of everything shared in this course, you'll start to identify markets, niches and opportunities on your own.

Maybe you'll start the next big grading company. Maybe you'll import Japanese cards to sell on the US market. Maybe you'll open the next big Pokemon website with thousands of cards.

We wish you well on your Pokemon journey and we're confident you'll be able to build a successful Pokemon business and crush the competition.

Stockroomdeals.com

www.ingramcontent.com/pod-product-compliance
Lightning Source LLC
Chambersburg PA
CBHW080446220526
45465CB00007B/2784